LORD, HEAR OUR CRY
A 30-Day Prayer Challenge

GRAHAM

P.O. Box 799070
Dallas, TX 75379
1-800-414-7693
jgraham@powerpoint.org
www.jackgraham.org

Unless otherwise indicated, Scripture verses quoted are
taken with permission from the English Standard Version.

INTRODUCTION

Perhaps you have experienced the rather embarrassing situation of talking to someone you thought was in the room, only to turn around and discover that at some point during your compelling monologue, the person had silently left the room. You were then left with the realization that, for some amount of time, you were wasting your breath, just droning on and on to yourself.

I've talked to many people who liken this experience to prayer. They see no point in devoting themselves to prayer because in their view, God has left the room, and their words are bouncing off the ceiling.

In actuality, nothing could be further from the truth. The God we serve is accessible to us. He is available and attentive. God is near and intent on receiving every prayer that we choose to pray. *"This is the confidence that we have in approaching God,"* 1 John 5:14 says, *"that if we ask anything according to his will, he hears us."*

So what does it take to get our prayers through the ceiling and into the very presence of Almighty God? How can we prevail in prayer so that our prayers are answered?

I want to submit to you that when we come before God in humility and sincerity seeking His face, He hears us. And when we are willing to exchange our fleeting, infrequent prayers for passionate, persistent prayers, we will find the provision we need.

My purpose in writing this book is to motivate you not only to return to prayer, but also to challenge you to pray boldly and consistently for 30 days. On certain days I will encourage you to write down specific prayers to the Lord. (There are Prayer Pages provided in the back of this book to do so.)

More importantly as you embark on this journey to reignite your prayer life, I pray that God would open the eyes and ears of your heart so that you may truly experience once-and-for-all the *reason* for prayer, your *responsibility* in prayer, and the *results* you will experience when prayer is an essential part of your life.

Whether you consider yourself a committed

intercessor or a novice at prayer, use this time to reflect on the quality of your communication with the Lord. If you take this 30-day prayer challenge seriously, I truly believe that one month from now your life and the lives of those you love will be changed!

"The Lord is far from the wicked, but he hears the prayer of the righteous" (Proverbs 15:29).

—Jack Graham

SECTION ONE:
THE REASON FOR PRAYER

Over the years I've been asked a question about prayer many times: "If God already knows our thoughts and our needs, why should we pray?" In section one of *Lord, Hear Our Cry*, my desire is to help you understand the exciting, enriching experience of prayer and the great power available to you through prayer.

Prayer is an open invitation that Jesus offers; not simply to the super-saints or the spiritually elite. Every follower of Jesus, every child of the heavenly Father, is welcomed into

His presence through prayer.

Prayer is not a magic formula, a good luck wish, or some kind of spiritual lottery. Instead, it is a vital, living relationship with God. It is a promise for believers and an avenue through which we receive what God desires to give. Our heavenly Father waits for us and welcomes us when we are in His presence in prayer. With that encouragement in mind, let's examine the biblical reasons for prayer.

DAY 1:
THE PURPOSE OF PRAYER

For this reason I bow my knees before the Father.
—Ephesians 3:14

At its core, Christianity is all about the *relationship* between God and those whom He created. But because God is spirit in nature, we can't relate to Him as we would a friend whom we can see and hear and meet for coffee on a Tuesday afternoon. No, the way we commune with God—the vehicle for fellowship with Him—is prayer.

In the same way you would foster a relationship with another human through quality time and communication, you can strengthen your relationship with God by communicating frequently with Him through prayer. You can learn of God's character through prayer. You can learn of His preferences, His plans for your life, and His activity in the world by prayer. And it is by prayer that you can play a role in His ushering heaven down to earth.

Too often we view prayer as transactional—we pray only when we need God's help with a specific problem. For example, a loved one becomes ill or we run into financial trouble so we call out to God to help us in that specific situation. While God certainly hears these requests, His deepest desire is to have *ongoing* fellowship with us through prayer.

Years ago I was shown a very simple diagram illustrating the purpose of prayer. At the top was the throne of God, and at the bottom were followers of Christ. On the right-hand side was a steady stream of plans that God wished to accomplish on earth, and on the left-hand side, a steady stream of prayers, prayed by faithful men and women of God.

The implication of the image was this: the essence of prayer is a loop in which our heavenly Father, by His Spirit, places requests and petitions on our hearts, only for us to offer them back to Him. What begins in heaven returns to heaven, via the mysterious power of prayer. In this way, prayer is not working to change our Father's mind; it is instead finding the mind of God.

I think most of us would say our prayer life

isn't what it ought to be. I encounter many committed Christians who have struggled with maintaining a regular prayer life. I pray this book will be a great encouragement and help to you as you seek to strengthen your prayer life and your relationship with God.

Set aside a specific time to pray today. Perhaps your first prayer could be, "Lord, I ask for Your help and Your divine power to assist me in faithfully and consistently praying over the next 30 days."

DAY 2:
THE NECESSITY OF PRAYER

Jesus looked at them and said, "With man it is impossible, but not with God. For all things are possible with God." —Mark 10:27

How many times, when faced with a difficult situation, do we manipulate, plan, scheme, dream, and yet do not pray? Sometimes we'd almost rather do anything than pray. Why pray when we can worry about it? Why pray when we can try to figure it out ourselves?

We must change our way of thinking about

prayer to realize that it is not an *obligation*; it is an *opportunity*. Prayer is not just a requirement; it is also a privilege and an invitation to experience the power of God. Prayer is spiritual breathing—our normal and natural experience in Christ.

The word *pray* that Jesus uses throughout the New Testament is the most simple and basic of all the words for prayer, and it means to "wish forward" or "to desire onward." God wants to hear the desires of our hearts. Psalm 37:4 says, *"Delight yourself in the Lord, and he will give you the desires of your heart."* God wants to hear what's on your heart! He wants to hear your desires and your dreams. He wants to hear about your failures as well as your successes.

Prayer is necessary because we need God. Situations will arise in this life that are humanly impossible to overcome. In those times we need wisdom, guidance, and direction from God. On a daily basis we need insight from God's Holy Spirit to discern His will and understand His Word. We need hope in dark times, strength in trials, and hope for eternity. Truly it is impossible to succeed in the Christian life apart from prayer.

I love the words of the old hymn, "What a Friend We Have in Jesus." The first stanza explains perfectly why prayer is a necessity in the life of the believer:

Oh, what peace we often forfeit;
Oh, what needless pain we bear.
All because we do not carry
Everything to God in prayer.[1]

You can pray anywhere, anytime about anything. Tell God about your needs. Pray

1 Scriven, Joseph M. "What a Friend We Have in Jesus," 1855.

for your family and your friends. Pray when you are in pain and when you're living in victory. Pray about your finances and your future. Beginning today, make prayer a non-negotiable, necessary part of your day.

———◇———

In your prayer time, think about each part of your life: your relationships, your occupation, your talents and hobbies, your health, and your future. Do you realize that each of these should be covered in prayer daily? Spend time today thanking God for the unique life situation in which He's placed you.

DAY 3:
THE COMMAND TO PRAY

*And he told them a parable to the effect
that they ought always to pray and not lose heart.*
—Luke 18:1

I n Luke 11:2, as Jesus was about to instruct the disciples on how to pray, He began with, *"When you pray."* Notice that Jesus said, *"when,"* not *"if."*

We are commanded to pray. Prayer is a demonstration of our obedience to God. It is one the essentials of the Christian life.

Prayer is also an opportunity to receive from our heavenly Father all that He desires to give.

It is amazing to me that we struggle in the area of prayer when God has promised so much. When you and I arrive at heaven's gate someday, no doubt we will be shocked by our lack of faithfulness as it relates to prayer. We will see firsthand the vast storehouse of blessing God had reserved for us, if only we had asked for His intervention in our lives. *"You do not have because you do not ask"* James 4:2 says. What a fitting reminder to pray while we still have life left to live! Indeed, nothing good, nothing great, nothing lasting, nothing holy can ever happen apart from prayer.

It has been said that we can do more than pray after we pray, but we cannot do more than pray until we pray. No person comes to faith in Jesus Christ apart from believing prayer. This is because when we believe in the power of prayer we are acknowledging the omnipotence, holiness, compassion and deity of God the Father. No person transforms the culture in which we live apart from prayer. No person serves as a committed disciple, a compelling witness, an effective parent, or a loving spouse apart from the power of prayer. It is prayer alone that yields fruitfulness in life because it is prayer that connects us to God.

That is why prayer should never be a sideline habit for believers. Prayer should not just be a ritual performed at the beginning of a family meal. We are to pray, persistently and passionately in dependence and in obedience. And let me be clear, if you are not praying, there is no way you can ever grow as a Christian. Without prayer, there is no way you will ever truly know God intimately. Prayer flows out of a life connected to Christ. And prayer also connects our life to Christ.

Pause for a moment and think about your prayer life. Are you communicating with God regularly through prayer? If not, when was the last time you prayed? What do you think is standing in the way of your praying more often?

In your prayer time today, ask God to give you an even deeper desire to pray.

DAY 4:
KNOWING GOD THROUGH PRAYER

*"Oh Lord, God of heaven, the great and awesome
God, who keeps his covenant of love with those
who love him and obey his commandments,
let your ear be attentive and your eyes opened
to hear the prayer your servant is praying."*
—Nehemiah 1:5–6

The verse above gives us an incredible
glimpse into the prayer life of Nehemiah.
These powerful words reveal Nehemiah's
steadfast belief in the power of God. He's able to
pray with conviction because he knows that his

God is in control. Even as Nehemiah learned of the destruction of Jerusalem's walls and faced the seemingly impossible task of rebuilding them, he knew that God was still on His throne.

In the same way, knowing God builds your trust in Him. It is through knowing God that our eyes are opened to see ourselves, and the world around us, from His perspective. If you want to know God in a deeper, more meaningful way, if you want to grow in your relationship with Him, start with prayer.

As you begin to discern the character of God through prayer, you will realize that God can handle any problem in your life. Do you believe that? God is bigger and greater than any situation, any crisis in your life!

That's what Nehemiah believed. He had faith in

a great and mighty God. Through his prayer he was saying, "Lord, I know you can handle this!"

For some believers today, it is challenging to see God as loving, caring, and available because they have grown up in homes where their father was the opposite of these things. *If my heavenly Father is anything like my earthly father,* they think, *then I want nothing to do with Him.* If that is true for you, please be encouraged: your heavenly Father will never let you down. He is at all times loving and tender; He is compassionate and kind. He longs with deep-seated affection to relate with you as the best father would relate with his son.

When you know God and He knows you—when tragedy comes, when sorrow knocks at your door, when you're in the middle of a crisis—you won't have to panic because He will already be there in your life. Don't be a stranger to prayer.

In your prayer time today, ask God to reveal Himself—His true nature and character—to you. If applicable, use a Prayer Page to write down any feelings of disappointment, discouragement, or uncertainty that may be hindering your relationship with God. Offer these things to your Heavenly Father in prayer, asking Him to heal and remove these "roadblocks" from your heart.

DAY 5:
HEARING FROM GOD
THROUGH PRAYER

"Let me hear in the morning of your steadfast love, for in you I trust. Make me know the way I should go, for to you I lift up my soul." —Psalm 143:8

I've been told by my wife and others that I am a "Type A" personality. Supposedly Type A's are hard-charging, competitive, multi-taskers. While these qualities can be positive, I have to keep my natural tendencies under control. Because if I'm not careful, I can enter every day on my agenda and my schedule, doing only what I think is right.

That is why I endeavor each day to take time to listen to God. A sound relationship, after all, is a two-way street. Prayer should be a conversation, a dialogue between a child and a Father, between a friend and a Heavenly Friend. So we must make sure that we take time to listen. As important as it is to pray and to record our prayers, it is every bit as important to listen to the Lord.

In Scripture, young Samuel understood how to stop and listen for God's voice. He didn't pray, "Listen, Lord, for your servant is *speaking*." No, he prayed, "Speak, Lord, for your servant is *listening*!" (1 Samuel 3:10) It will do us well to follow suit.

It's a difficult concept to define, this idea of "hearing" the voice of God. But this much I know to be true: When we pray, asking for God's guidance, He is faithful to direct our steps. He might open or close a door. He might speak to us through a friend. He might prompt in us some word or deed that we never would have discovered ourselves. John 10:27 says, *"My sheep hear my voice, and I know them, and they follow me."*

And so, we pray. We tell God with sincere hearts that we desire to pursue His will. We ask Him with boldness and great belief to speak to our hearts and shape our ways.

When you delight yourself in God, when you look to Him, listen to Him, and linger in His presence, then God begins to implant His desires on your heart. He begins to change your desires to match His.

To put ourselves in the best position to hear from God, we need to set aside a quiet time every day—a time preferably at the beginning of the day—to be alone with God in order to listen to Him, speak with Him, and open His Word.

In my own quiet, prayerful time, I make sure that I'm on God's agenda and not just on my own agenda. In prayer I slow down long enough to get my marching orders for the day. Prayer not only changes *things*, it changes me. It changes my attitude, it changes my priorities, and it gets my life in sync with God's plan.

Today, spend time listening for God. Ask Him to reshape your desires so they match His own.

DAY 6:
STRENGTHENING YOUR FAITH
THROUGH PRAYER

"Call to me and I will answer you,
and will tell you great and unsearchable things
you do not know." —Jeremiah 33:3

I love Jeremiah 33:3. I've heard some people call it "God's telephone number." Promises like this one contained throughout God's Word give us assurance and confidence that, when God's children pray, the Heavenly Father listens. He invites us to come to Him.

That is a staggering thought isn't it? God hears our prayers. While most of us have been told all of our lives that God answers prayer, that fact just blows right by us most of the time. Think about this: if it is true that God Almighty, the Creator of the universe, is interested in hearing from us and answers our prayers according to His perfect will for our lives, then that is the most amazing thing we could possibly experience! And that's why it is absolutely ludicrous that we don't pray as we ought to pray.

From Genesis to Revelation, we can read the prayers of the heroes of our faith: the prayers of Abraham and Moses, David and Solomon, Hannah and Mary, Jesus and Paul, and so many others. These men and women were connected to God through prayer. And their prayers are recorded for us to show us that God hears our prayers!

It is encouraging to know that we are not heard because of the language of our prayers, the length of our prayers, or the logic of our prayers, but because of the life that prays before God. It's not your words that matter; it is the genuineness of your heart. God is listening for people whose lives are transparent before Him, who are laid out before Him. God is looking for honest, genuine prayer. But most of all He wants to see your faith.

In Luke 18:13 Jesus tells the story of a tax collector who simply cried out, "God be merciful to me a sinner!" and in doing so, gave one of the most powerful prayers in the Bible. He demonstrated the most basic level of belief and faith by simply crying out to the One who could meet his needs. Jesus said this man got God's attention and went home justified.

As your prayer life increases, so will your faith and trust in the God who loves you and can meet your deepest needs.

Today, put aside any desire to say the "right words," and just be honest before God. Tell Him what is on your heart, confess any fears or anxiety you may be experiencing. Don't forget to thank Him for the blessings you have in your life.

DAY 7:
SEEKING FORGIVENESS
THROUGH PRAYER

If we confess our sins, he is faithful and just to forgive us our sins and to cleanse us from all unrighteousness. —1 John 1:9

Did you know that unconfessed sin could keep God from hearing your prayers? It's not that He doesn't want to hear us; it's just that God, in His perfect holiness, cannot come near to sin. The sin must first be removed.

David prayed in Psalm 66:18, *"If I had cherished*

iniquity in my heart, the Lord would not have listened." In other words, if we practice sin habitually without repentance, God will not hear us. Of all the promises for answered prayer, here's a promise for God *not* to answer prayer.

We can't expect God to bless our lives and those we are praying for if our hearts are overrun with hate and malice. In Matthew chapter 5, Jesus says that if there's an unresolved conflict between you and another believer, go first and settle that conflict and then come and pray. Sin is serious business to God, and therefore should be serious business to us. If there's anything clogging the channel of prayer in our lives then we need to come to the Lord, confess our sins, and receive forgiveness.

The Bible explains that we are all sinners in

need of cleansing. We have fallen short of God's perfect standard and suffer from that fallen state each day. Throughout Scripture, sin is described as a disease that produces spiritual death. It is no wonder, then, that the psalmist cried out, *"Wash me thoroughly, God!"*[2] When we are honest about our own sinfulness, we will crave God's cleansing ways.

There may be some of you who are thinking, *I would be an absolute hypocrite to pray. I've gone too far and done too much to receive forgiveness.* Let me remind you that there is rejoicing in heaven when one sinner repents.[3] It's time to quit beating yourself down and get away from your guilt. Make today the day to repent of your sin and respond to the forgiveness made possible through Christ.

We can forever come to the Father because of

2 Psalm 51:2 3 Luke 15:10

what Christ has done for us. We have been forgiven and freed. We have been changed and cleansed and set on the path of everlasting communion with God.

Clear your conscience before connecting with God through prayer, and you'll find that when you do pray, you'll experience greater confidence and greater power.

---◇---

Today, ask God to help you move forward in forgiveness. Do you need to give forgiveness to another person or receive it from God? Ask God to search your heart and reveal any sin that may be a barrier between your prayers and Him.

DAY 8:
GAINING PERSPECTIVE
THROUGH PRAYER

Now the end of all things is at hand; therefore be self-controlled and sober-minded for the sake of your prayers. —1 Peter 4:7

If you have ever played in a football game, you know that when you're down on the field, you can't see all of the plays developing. Your view is limited to what is happening immediately around you. On the other hand, if you're an offensive coordinator for a football team, you are able to go up to the press box and look down on the entire field. From this vantage point you can clearly see what the defense and offense are doing.

In the same way, sometimes we're too close to our own problems; we're right in the middle, and we can't see what is happening. We need a clearer vision, a new perspective. And so what do we need to do? We need to get up higher! We need to get lifted up into the presence of the Lord and gain a new perspective in finding God's will and His wisdom in our lives.

Prayer is what changes our perspective in life. It transforms our view of everything that we do. And when we humble ourselves in prayer and hunger more for God, we will discover a life filled with spiritual breakthroughs and benefits.

God desires to reveal His perspective and impart

His wisdom to us. James 1:5 says, *"If any of you lacks wisdom, let him ask God, who gives generously to all without reproach, and it will be given him."*

When we yield our lives to God, we can live in peace and with a proper perspective. We can go forward knowing that every detail is under His command and under His control. So, whether we're praying for healing or praying for a house, we're praying in the will of God. We're praying, "Lord if you heal me, my body is Your body. Lord if you give me this house, this house is Your house." That's praying with godly perspective.

Prayer is the key to maintaining a godly perspective. And with this correct perspective of God's will for our lives we can place our confidence in the One *"who is able to do far more*

abundantly than all that we ask or think, according to the power at work within us." (Ephesians 3:20).

Prayerfully consider the problem that is most troubling in your life today. As you lift it up in prayer to the Lord, ask for His help in viewing the situation from His perspective—as an all-knowing, powerful, omnipresent God. Write this situation down on a Prayer Page and leave space to record any insights God provides in the days to come.

DAY 9:
RECEIVING GOD'S PROVISION
THROUGH PRAYER

My God shall supply all of your needs
according to His riches in glory in Jesus Christ.
—Philippians 4:19

In the Lord's Prayer, our model prayer, we
are directed to ask our Father in Heaven
for daily provision, daily "bread." Rather than
trusting that it will show up again and again
we must realize that we are dependent upon
the Lord.

God is not only interested in our spiritual lives, He is interested in our physical and material lives as well. So prayer is not only for God's heavenly glory, but prayer is provided for our earthly good.

Now, it may not seem all that spiritual to ask God for "bread," but we must keep in mind that His meaning here addresses not just physical bread, but also bread of the spiritual sort. When we pray, "Give us this day our daily bread" we are expressing our dependence on God and conveying our gratitude for His gracious provision in our lives.

Truly, no matter how hard we work, how much we earn, and how cleverly we invest and save and buy, all that we have is a gift from His hand. Every good thing comes from God.

Praying for daily bread reminds us to live one day at a time.

This exhortation references an Old Testament story about the children of Israel being led to the Promised Land and receiving manna—or bread—from God one day at a time. Each morning, they would find manna covering the ground and were instructed to gather up just enough for that particular day. If they tried to gather up more than that day's needs and store it for the next day, the manna would mysteriously spoil. It was an object lesson for the Israelites that carries significance for our lives as well: we are to come to God daily, living by His provision from hand to mouth.

Psalm 37:25 reveals that David knew something about depending upon the Lord for daily needs.

He said: *"I have been young, and now am old, yet I have not seen the righteous forsaken or his children begging for bread."*

When we are persistent in prayer for our daily provision, God is pleased to provide for us. This puts us in a position of reliance upon God and fills our hearts with gratitude!

What is your greatest need today? Bring it to God in prayer and record that need on a Prayer Page with today's date. Leave space next to your request to record the date and the way in which God provided for your need.

DAY 10:
ASKING FOR GOD'S PROTECTION THROUGH PRAYER

God is our refuge and strength, a very present help in trouble. —Psalm 46:1

S amuel Chadwick, a great Christian of yesteryear, once said: "The one concern of the devil is to keep Christians from praying. He fears nothing from prayerless studies, prayerless work, and prayerless religion. He laughs at our toil and mocks our wisdom, but he trembles when we pray."[4]

---

4 Samuel Chadwick in Draper's Book of Quotations for the Christian World, comp. Edythe Draper (Wheaton: Tyndale, 1992), 493-94.

There is a wrestling match we're involved in, my friend, and our opponent, Satan, doesn't like to lose. Incidentally, if you've never sensed the devil's work in your life, perhaps it is because you are walking in the same direction as he is! Turn around and begin walking with Christ, and I guarantee you'll meet him face-to-face.

This may seem like a cause for trepidation in your life, but you need not fear Satan's assault. Each time we engage in spiritual battle with the enemy of our souls, we seize a grand opportunity for spiritual growth—in our minds, in our hearts, and in our lives. We become more vigilant about praying for power to defeat him and as a result, step into the next spiritual battle much stronger than we were before.

In this sense, prayer is not only worship and work, prayer is warfare! That is why God gave us a powerful weapon in prayer—prayer as a covering, prayer as a source of strength, and prayer as a means to stand firm in the fiercest battles!

In praying for protection, we come before God, requesting for Him to serve as our shield, our strength, our fortress, our deliverer, our strong tower, and a very present help in time of need. When we pray protection, we do so humbly in recognition of our weakness and vulnerability.

In contrast, when we fail to pray for protection, we are allowing pride and arrogance to direct us. It is for this reason that 1 Corinthians 10:12 tells us, *"let anyone who thinks that he stands take heed lest he fall."*

We need God's strength and protection every

day to combat the devil's schemes. It is foolish to enter into battle without protection, especially when God has given us specific weapons for our warfare. Prayer is the invisible energy, the invisible force that is the key to victory.

Spend your prayer time today praying a covering of protection upon yourself and those closest to you.

SECTION TWO:
THE RESPONSIBILITY OF PRAYER

Prayer is hard work; it is a mental and spiritual discipline. In order to improve our prayer life, we must practice the exercise of prayer. Thankfully, knowing our weaknesses, God provided the perfect prayer partner. God's Holy Spirit enables us and encourages us when we pray. In Scripture, prayer and the Holy Spirit are inseparably linked together.

Prayer enables us to bring our burdens and our battles to the Lord and receive the strength and help we need. All the resources of God are available to us in prayer. If we could just realize how our Lord longs to answer our petitions, how much more would we pray?

God is the One with the answers; it is He alone who can meet our deepest needs. Whatever your requests may be—strength, guidance, a job, renewed health, a helpmate in life—as a child of God, you can bring it to your Father.

With this assurance, we approach God asking for our answers to our prayers. But can we be sure that we are praying correctly and effectively? Let's see what God's Word says about our responsibilities in prayer.

DAY 11:
MAKE PRAYER A PRIORITY

But seek first the kingdom of God and His righteousness, and all of these things will be added unto you. —Matthew 6:33

I've heard it said that the first 10 or 15 minutes of each day really determine how the rest of your day will go. And if you begin your day in prayer, acknowledging God as first in your life, you are making a wise choice.

Before I get out of bed every morning, I lift my heart to the Lord and say, "God, I praise You. I want You to have my ambitions, my attention, my life, and my all this day!"

Too often, rather than putting Jesus Christ first in our lives, we allow many other thoughts and "things" to consume us. But Scripture reminds us that anything we love more, serve more, or worship more than Jesus Himself is idolatry, plain and simple! Jesus will not share His place of Lordship in our lives. So before you pray, before you start asking, make sure that you're practicing the principle of putting God first.

I know life can be busy. I know obligations must be met. I'm just suggesting that before we tend to our responsibilities, we should devote ourselves to God in prayer. I need that, and so do you.

Imagine a friend telling you of a great struggle

he is facing in life and saying, "Well, I guess the only thing left to do is pray," to which you think to yourself, *Oh, my goodness has it come down to that?* Rather than treating prayer as a last resort, begin to consider prayer as the holy privilege that it is.

Each of us needs a set-aside, set-apart encounter with the living God at key moments throughout our day in order to navigate this thing called life. There can be no answered prayers until we're willing to spend time kneeling before God to receive what He delights and desires to give. Keeping our focus on God through prayer reaps great rewards.

So what about you? Are you making prayer a priority in your life? Do you give Jesus the first thoughts of your day? Before your feet hit the floor, do you lift your heart up to God in adoration and praise, thanking Him for the light of a new day?

---◇---

Tomorrow, make it a point to begin your day in prayer. Use a Prayer Page to write down the first thoughts you have when you wake up. Then, ask God for guidance in these areas of your life.

DAY 12:
BRING EVERY SITUATION TO GOD

Cast your burden on the LORD and he will sustain you; he will never permit the righteous to be moved. —Psalm 55:22

The first thing we should do when we have a problem or a need, is to turn it over to God—not as our last chance, but as our first choice!

A perfect example of this can be found in Acts chapter four which describes a scene following Christ's Resurrection when Peter and John were arrested and put on trial for preaching the

Gospel. They were threatened, within an inch of their lives, by the same angry crowd that had crucified Jesus. Finally they were released, but only after being sternly warned "not to speak or teach at all in the name of Jesus." Those who opposed Christ figured the only way to stop the Gospel was to shut up those who were preaching it.

In light of the threats against them, do you know what Peter and John did? They prayed. They gathered with fellow believers and prayed these words, *"And now, Lord, look upon their threats and grant to your servants to continue to speak your Word with all boldness"* (4:29). Instead of panicking, instead of fretting, they immediately handed over their problem to the Lord.

Isn't it interesting that they didn't pray for

safety or protection against these threats? Because they trusted God completely they were able to say, "Lord, here is an impossible situation. Here are these threats against us. We trust you to help us." I especially love the end of verse 29 that says: *"and grant to Your servants boldness to continue speaking Your word!"* These men had no intention of giving up and giving in to defeat!

But there is even more good news in this story. As Peter and John lifted their prayers to the Lord, the place in which they were gathered began to shake! (4:31) It was revival power moving! It was God moving! Revival happens when God shows up in our midst.

What happened in this visible, physical manifestation of God needs to happen to us spiritually. Some of us need to be shaken! And when we pray and surrender our lives to the Lord, we can be sure that He will shake us and stir us, waking us from our lethargy and our lukewarmness. When we bring every situation before the Lord in prayer, He will hear our cries and respond with heavenly power.

Are you ready to take your hands off the problem that's heaviest on your heart today and hand it over to God? Use a Prayer Page to write down something you have been struggling with and have not given to God. Now, pray about it.

DAY 13:
PRAY WITH A SINCERE HEART

"If my people who are called by my name humble
themselves, and pray and seek my face and
turn from their wicked ways, then I will hear
from heaven and will forgive their sin and heal
their land." —2 Chronicles 7:14

As children of God, we must constantly monitor our heart's posture to be sure our motivation for entering His presence is pure.

If you're a parent, then you know how deflating it can be for your kids to constantly beg you for toys or permission to do fun things. Don't you wish they would crawl into your lap sometimes just to say, "I love you"? Having a sincere heart before God means refraining from running into His presence with each day's shopping list and instead slowly, quietly, humbly expressing gratitude for who He is.

While prayer is a joyful experience, it is also a serious encounter with God! We should come before a God with an understanding of our reverence before Him.

Sincere prayer is not about the physical position in which you pray but about the spiritual attitude of your heart. When Paul prayed, he did so as a submissive son to a Father. When Nehemiah prayed, he referred to himself as God's servant. He asked God to be with him and to guide him as he acted in obedience to God's will.

In Matthew 6, Jesus rebukes a group of people, calling them hypocrites for praying to be seen by others instead of praying to bring honor to God. *"They have received their reward,"* Jesus said. *"But when you pray, go into your room and shut the door and pray to your Father who is in secret. And your Father who sees in secret will reward you"* (vv. 5–6).

What Jesus is pointing to here is the insincerity of some people's prayers. Yes, they may be saying prayers, but they're certainly not praying prayers. And there is a vast difference between the two. When people offer repetitious prayers as a matter of routine, in a vain attempt to perform for God, inside, their hearts are unmoved.

The only way I know how to identify this in my life is to ask myself, do I only pray when people are watching? Do I simply pray so others will think more of me? Jesus is asking about our motivation.

So how about you? What's your prayer life like— not what others see, but what God sees? What is your attitude when you pray? Are you resisting Him, demanding your own way? Or are you bowing before Him and saying, as Jesus said, "Not as I will, but as you will"? Is it your desire, truly, to draw near to God, to know Him, to please Him?

Read and meditate on Psalm 139:23 in your prayer time today: *"Search me, O God, and know my heart! Try me and know my thoughts."*

DAY 14:
PRAY CONSTANTLY

Rejoice always, pray without ceasing, give thanks in all circumstances; for this is the will of God in Christ Jesus for you. —1 Thessalonians 5:16–18

I often encounter a misconception about prayer that I call the salt-shaker principle. Namely that a little prayer here, a little prayer there—like we're seasoning our food with salt—should be enough. I'm here to tell you that a little "seasoning" is not enough. We need to saturate our lives in prayer!

In fact, we're told that we're to pray at all times about all things; that our lives should be lived with a continual, abiding attitude of prayerful devotion and dependence upon God. As followers of Christ, we ought always to be a mere breath away from prayer. But I've discovered in my own life that I won't pray "anywhere and everywhere" until I first pray somewhere.

Many times we become discouraged because we just don't know what else to say to the Lord. If our prayer is a monologue, we won't last very long as we pray! We must remember that prayer is not just saying things to God. Prayer is also listening to God.

When we stay long enough at the place of prayer, God is able to speak to us and clarify

His will, teaching us what to pray. *"And he who searches hearts knows what is the mind of the Spirit, because the Spirit intercedes for the saints according to the will of God"* (Romans 8:27).

So what does it look like to pray without ceasing? It means to pray as often as we can, about everything that we can.

A habit is something we can't stop doing— something we do constantly. And our habits, once we form them, form us. But not all habits are bad! We are told in the Scripture that the vital habit of the believer should be prayer. We should cultivate the habit of prayer, and make it a "habit" of our hearts. And certainly the more we do something, the better we get at it.

When was the last time you missed a meal because you prayed? When was the last time you prayed late into the night because you were burdened? When was the last time you got up early in the morning because you need to seek the face of God?

Nehemiah prayed with that kind of passion. He prayed with that kind of heart, desire, and persistence. And in turn, God answered his prayers in mighty ways.

Today, make it your mission to pray as often as you can. Don't worry if your prayers are not lengthy or well-thought out. Just keep the lines of communication open with God all day. Talk to Him as you would to a close friend.

DAY 15:
PRAY PERSISTENTLY

Continue steadfastly in prayer, being watchful in it with thanksgiving. —Colossians 4:2

Persistent prayer takes faithfulness and patience. Because typically we're praying about things in our lives that are slow to change. If you're knocking on the doors of heaven now, in anticipation of God answering a real request in your life, be assured that He hears you. God knows your need, and He cares.

In Luke 11:5–10, Jesus offers an interesting

lesson in persistence through a parable: *"Which of you who has a friend will go to him at midnight and say to him, 'Friend, lend me three loaves, for a friend of mine has arrived on a journey, and I have nothing to set before him'; and he will answer from within, 'Do not bother me; the door is now shut, and my children are with me in bed. I cannot get up and give you anything'? I tell you, though he will not get up and give him anything because he is his friend, yet because of his impudence he will rise and give him whatever he needs. And I tell you, ask, and it will be given to you; seek, and you will find; knock, and it will be opened to you. For everyone who asks receives, and the one who seeks finds, and to the one who knocks it will be opened."*

Here, Jesus sets the stage for how His followers are to make their requests known to God. He is not suggesting that we must beg God in the sense of forcing His hand. In fact, it is the opposite. Jesus is showing us that God desires to give good things to His children, unlike the man who was reluctant to help his friend.

When the answer to our heartfelt plea is slow in coming we must persevere. Persistent prayer means praying through our doubt, praying through our fears, and refusing to give up. So many times we pray for certain things to happen, when God has a better plan in mind. And so we keep knocking until we receive the direction we need.

Scripture says that God will reward in heaven those who are faithful to pray here on earth,[5] because it is these devoted people who have the greatest eternal impact. Praying believers change the destinies of men and women and even the

5 Matthew 6:17-18.

histories of nations. I firmly believe that when we get to heaven, we'll see countless rewards given to people who never preached from a platform, who were never identified as great leaders, but who prayed faithfully, without fail.

Have you ever "given up" on a prayer request thinking that God won't answer? Let me encourage you today with the qualities of our awesome God: He is patient, long-suffering, and all-knowing. Will you trust Him today with a long-term prayer request? Will you commit to praying persistently about what's on your heart until you hear from God?

DAY 16:
PRAY BOLDLY

Let us therefore come boldly unto the throne of grace, that we may obtain mercy and find grace to help in time of need. —Hebrews 4:16, KJV

I believe that we have become too complacent in our prayers. We pray too many safe, vague, and repetitive prayers.

When we don't understand the purpose and the value of prayer, our natural tendency is to be lazy, praying things such as, "God, bless my friends, and bless my family. Amen." But general prayers solicit general answers, and we rarely see God moving in the generalities of our lives. His movement is detected in the details, in the specifics of our days. Pray in such a way that when God answers your prayer, you know without question what He said!

Praying with boldness is a not a "Now I lay me down to sleep" kind of praying. It is not "God bless our food" kind of praying! Bold praying is militant praying, mighty praying in the name of Jesus! Bold prayer is the mountain-moving means by which we connect with the will of Almighty God.

If you've never been personal and precise with God, I encourage you to abandon "safe" prayers and take a risk for once. He already knows what we need. He knows the desires of our hearts. And He loves for us to shoot straight with Him, as sons and daughters to a loving Father above.

In my experience, God does business with those who mean business with Him. So away with half-hearted, heartless prayer! May we pray shamelessly and with great passion. It costs blood, sweat, and tears to pray boldly, to bruise your knuckles, asking, seeking, and knocking. But it's worth it because when we pray, God moves!

I know this: the only prayer that God does not answer is the prayer that you don't ask! We learn from Jesus that we are to pray passionately, desperately, fervently, and when the situation demands it; big, bold, audacious prayer!

It is important to note that boldness is

not brashness, nor arrogance. Boldness is openness and confidence. Boldness flows from our unwavering confidence in the Gospel. Look back at Hebrews 4:16 on the previous page. This verse is telling us that when we come *boldly* to the throne of God we can store up grace and mercy for times of need. And when that time comes, we can be confident that God will hear us.

Envision yourself approaching Jesus with your prayers today. He is our High Priest who welcomes you into His presence and receives your requests. What is on your heart today?

DAY 17:
PRAY USING SCRIPTURE

"If you abide in Me, and My words abide in you, you will ask what you desire, and it will be done for you." —John 15:7

In the Christian life there is a beautiful and healthy balance between the Word of God and prayer. In prayer we speak to God. In Bible study God speaks to us. We are to store up God's Word in our hearts in order that we might know His will.

It's impossible to know what God wants us

to *do* until we first know what God has *said* in His Word. Because so much of the will of God has been revealed in the Bible, we must invest time reading and meditating upon the Word of God. And as we do, we'll discover deeper aspects of God's will—promises we've never before relied on, avenues we've never journeyed along, open doors we've never seen. Psalm 119:105 calls God's Word *"a lamp unto our feet and a light unto our path."*

While it may not be feasible to study God's Word all day long, we can reflect on what we have read as we go about our day. When we do so, God will bring to remembrance the promises we need. God has no favorites, but certainly, He does have friends. And by revealing Himself in new ways to faithful students of His Word, He shares intimate secrets with those friends.

God loves it when we call upon Him using His own Word. He has blessed His Word not only when it is preached and proclaimed, but also when it is prayed. The most effective prayer is one filled with God's Word.

Over the years I have learned how to pray the Scriptures by making them personal. For example, Proverbs 3:5–6 is a passage that I've loved through the years: *"Trust the Lord with all your heart and lean not on your own understanding. In all your ways acknowledge Him and He will direct your path."*

Here is how I would pray that verse: "Lord, I trust You with all my heart. Help me not to lean on my own understanding. I'm going to acknowledge You in all my ways. And I know that You, Lord, will direct my path."

That's praying the Scriptures. That's making a Scripture promise your own promise.

If you need God to come through in a powerful way to meet a need in your life, pray Philippians 4:19 like this: "Lord, I know that You are my God and that You will supply my every need according to Your riches in glory in Jesus Christ."

Open God's Word today and find a biblical promise that speaks to your heart. Write it down and then use it to create a personal prayer to the Lord.

DAY 18:
PRAY FOR OTHERS

First of all, then, I urge that supplications, prayers, intercessions, and thanksgivings be made for all people, for kings and all who are in high positions, that we may lead a peaceful and quiet life, godly and dignified in every way. This is good, and it is pleasing in the sight of God our Savior, who desires all people to be saved and to come to the knowledge of the truth. —1 Timothy 2:1–4

P erhaps one of the greatest ways to experience the power of prayer is through intercession—praying for others. Intercession is the graduate level of prayer.

The Bible names several specific groups of people for whom we are to pray.

- Those in public leadership. This includes the President and Congress, our national leaders, our state and local government leaders, police officers, teachers, and others in authority. Whether or not we agree with their policies and opinions, we are to pray for them—that they would come to saving faith in Jesus Christ.

- Our spiritual leaders. The devil aims his biggest guns at God's leaders, and today, many are discouraged, hurting, and even falling into sin. God's people need to pray for God's leaders. I ask you from the depths of my heart to pray for the pastors, missionaries, and Christian leaders in America and throughout the world.

- The lost. Are you praying for those in your life who do not know Jesus? Prayer is the means by which we help point others to faith in Christ. You and I know people who have yet to receive God's gift of grace, and the first step we ought to take is to commit the matter to prayer. Only God, by His Spirit, can reach a neighbor, rescue a prodigal child, and turn a wayward heart toward Him. By devoting ourselves to persistent prayer, we join Him in that noble work.

- Our country. We need to cry out to God and pray for our country. And if you love this country you will pray for God to revive His Church. Pray that God would renew our families and our communities. We need to pray for our fellow citizens and our neighbors, and turn our prayers to action. Psalm 33:2 says, *"Blessed is the nation whose God is the LORD."* Let us join in prayer that our nation will return to its roots of honoring God.

Today, devote a Prayer Page to intercessory prayer. As you pray, consider world, national, and local leaders, pastors, teachers, and those in military service. Then make a separate list of specific friends and acquaintances in your life who need to know Jesus.

Note: for more intercessory prayer ideas, see the 7 Centers of Influence Prayer Page in the back of this book.

DAY 19:
PRAY FOR GOD'S WILL TO BE DONE

"Your kingdom come. Your will be done on earth as it is in heaven." —Matthew 7:10

It's important to note that God's will is not always done on earth as it is in heaven. If that were the case, we wouldn't be encouraged to pray for heaven to invade earth, right? It is obvious that we live in a world that is suffering the consequences of grave sin, and that while God is sovereign over all, His will often is not accomplished in our midst. Murder, hatred, terrorism, divorce—these and a thousand other manifestations of our brokenness were never part of God's plan, which is why Jesus implores us to pray for the Father's will to be done. We must discover that it is God's will (and not ours) that is flawless, good, and true.

Prayer is not getting *our* will done in heaven, it is getting *God's* will done on earth. Our God is neither finite or erring or sinful. He is a perfect Heavenly Father who desires the best for His children. He will always give to us exactly what we need in His own way, in His own time.

Nothing lies outside the reach of prayer except that which lies outside the will of God. When we engage in seeking prayer, we tap into the greatest power source available to humankind, the power of God's will in the world.

The prayer life of the believer is not centered

around twisting God's arm or manipulating God's mind. But rather it is adjusting *our will* to the *will of God*. It is asking Him to help us bend *our* will to *His* will.

The Lord Jesus is the ultimate example of this. He said that it was his "food" or "nourishment" to do the will of the Father (see John 4:34). Jesus prayed, *"Father, if you are willing, remove this cup from me. Nevertheless, not my will, but yours, be done"* (Luke 22:42). And so we pray, seeking the will of God for our lives. God wants what is best for each one of us. The happiest and the best place on earth is right in the center of God's will.

It's been said that prayer is not changing God's mind but finding God's mind. So in seeking God and His will, we discover how to live. The way to learn what God wants with our lives is to pray.

1 John 5:14–15 says: *"Now this is the confidence that we have in Him, that if we ask anything according to His will, He hears us. And if we know that He hears us, whatever we ask, we know that we have the petitions that we have of Him."* We can pray with confidence and certainty in the will of God. Praying for the will of God is to pray for His glory in lives and when we get His glory we get our good.

Begin your prayer time by praying The Lord's Prayer today (see Matthew 6:9–13). Take time to soak in the meaning of each line. Pray specifically for God's will to be done on earth as it is in heaven.

DAY 20:
SEEK GOD'S WILL

Do not be conformed to this world, but be transformed by the renewal of your mind, that by testing you may discern what is the will of God, what is good and acceptable and perfect.
—Romans 12:2

I believe that so many have never discovered the power of prayer in seeking to know and do God's will. Step by step, day after day God reveals His will and shows the way to those who truly seek Him and ask Him. The Bible describes the will of God as "good and acceptable and perfect"—does it get any better than that?

I've met plenty of people who are nervous seeking the will of God in prayer because they want what *they want* and are anxious that what *God wants* for them involves an entirely different plan! What I tell them in response is that, God's will for our lives is what we *would* want if we really knew what we wanted.

And because most of us don't have the big picture of what is needed in our lives, we simply need to pray. We are to seek the will of God, something that we're to long for, love, yearn for, and yield to. Psalm 143:10 says, *"Teach me to do your will, for you are my God! Let your good Spirit lead me on level ground!"*

Not only are we to seek God's will, but we are to

practice the will of God. We don't come to God and say, "Lord, show me Your will and I'll decide whether or not I'm going to do it." No! Our attitude must be, "Your will, anytime, anywhere, any cost."

And so, we seek God's will through prayer. And then, upon sensing His direction, we joyfully follow it with grateful hearts, asking Him as we take each faith-filled step to bend our will to His perfect plan.

Seeking the will of God is asking that our lives be in conformity to His will. It is recognizing the sovereignty of God and saying, "Lord, your will is what I seek, your purpose, your plan in my life. I want to be on your agenda, not mine."

Jim Elliot, the martyred missionary, once wrote in his diary, "God always gives the best to those who leave the choice with Him." Wouldn't that be a marvelous way to live, allowing God to choose the course of our lives?

More than any other definition for success, I like this one best: "Success is the progressive realization of the will of God for our lives." Truer words have never been written.

Pray for the will of God in your life and make it your prayer every day. Real prayer is surrendering our will, to the will of God, submitting our way to the ways of God.

SECTION THREE:
THE RESULTS OF PRAYER

*"The prayer of a righteous person has great power
as it is working"* —James 5:16

God's very presence is recognized and released when we pray. And, yes, God still moves today in powerful, incredible ways! When we are faithful in our prayers, we will notice changes in our lives. Our fleshly desires will diminish in light of our desire to do God's will.

Prayer empowers us to be better friends, better spouses, better parents, better business partners, better people overall. The world will not understand why we are so different—why we know such joy in the face of adversity, why we feel such peace in a valley that's dark—but we'll know that the transformation we're experiencing is due solely to devoted prayer. The more time we spend on our knees in the presence of God, the more we will experience peace, hope, and joy filling our days.

In the final section of *Lord, Hear Our Cry*, we will learn of the incredible gifts God offers to those whose lives are centered around prayer.

DAY 21:
ANSWERS FROM GOD

Therefore the LORD waits to be gracious to you, and therefore he exalts himself to show mercy to you. For the LORD is a God of justice; blessed are all those who wait for him. —Isaiah 30:18

I f I were to take a poll asking people what they most want from prayer, I bet the number one response would be "answers." When we pray, we are seeking a response from God.

There is both human responsibility and divine reassurance that work in tandem to accomplish answered prayer. We humbly come before the throne of grace with our petitions, and God answers by faithfully directing our steps.

Knowing that God answers the prayers of those who love Him and are obedient to Him, it may be helpful to look at how He answers prayer:

- Sometimes God's answer is immediate. We pray and receive a "green light" from God. Doors open, things change, and we are certain of His hand in the situation.

- Sometimes the answer to prayer is delayed. We must always pray until God shows the way. It's also important to not get ahead of God. I've tried that a few times, and it never ended well. Isaiah 30:18 says, "the Lord waits to be gracious to you...blessed are all those who wait for him." Sometimes God is waiting to give us something more gracious than we can imagine. If our request is wrong, God says "no," if the timing is wrong, God says, "wait."

- Sometimes our requests are denied. When I hear people talk of "unanswered prayer," I want them to reconsider that phrase. Did God really not answer, or was His answer just, "no"? God always knows what is best for us, and we should be constantly thankful for His divine wisdom. Many of us have prayed for things in the past and now we're saying, whew, I'm glad that didn't happen!

For years, I've kept a journal of my prayers and God's answers to them. I can tell you this—when facing difficult circumstances, thumbing through these journals and seeing how God has faithfully answered, builds my confidence and faith. It reminds me that He will continue to provide for me.

If you have a pressing need today, know that God isn't holding out on you. Pray and wait for His answer.

Can you think of a time when God answered a specific prayer request of yours? Write it down. Now record three specific requests and include today's date. When you receive an answer from God, write a new date beside the old one.

DAY 22:
A HEART FOR OBEDIENCE

I desire to do your will, O my God;
your law is within my heart. —Psalm 40:8

When we are faithful to observe God's instruction for our lives, then He is faithful to bless us as only He can.

It's true, the "blessings" we receive may come in disguise—we gain humility from a job lay-off, we gain self-control from a dried-up bank account, we gain perseverance from a life-threatening illness—but we can be sure that our Father always has our best interest in mind.

The key here is obedience, the pattern of never falling away. It is our obedience that is divinely rewarded. It is our obedience that honors our God.

It is important to note that, prayer is not a *substitute* for obedience, nor is it an excuse for laziness. Throughout Scripture, when the people of God would pray, God would fill them, and then they would go in the name of Jesus and share their faith. They would become part of the solution to the problems that were all around them! Prayer makes us a part of the answer. That's why we need to arise from the place of prayer and with momentum move forward in spiritual service in obedience to God.

As a young preacher, I was so moved by the words of Steven Olford who said: "God is not responsible to lead us one step further than the measure of our obedience to him." In other words, God will not reveal more of His will to us if there are things we are not doing that He already has asked us to do. Our goal must not be the mere discovery of God's will; our goal must also be to *do* God's will.

When I get on my knees regularly and consistently to read God's Word and talk to God and listen to God, He always brings to mind things I can do bring glory to Him and to support the work of Christ. Our feet should be moved to action when we pray. That's obedience!

In contrast, instead of taking action in obedience, some people are always saying, "Well, I'm just waiting on the Lord to show me what I'm supposed to do. When He shows me, then I'll do it." These people are praying with no intention of getting right with God.

I've found in my own life that God's actually waiting on me most of the time. He's waiting on me to pray and to get up from that place of prayer and to act in the power of the Holy Spirit. Are you praying diligently and then responding to what God calls you to do?

Where can you be more obedient to God's call in your life? Has He placed a specific area of service on your heart? Use your prayer time today to ask God how He wants to use you in the work of His kingdom.

DAY 23:
DELIVERANCE FROM TEMPTATION

*"And lead us not into temptation, but deliver us from evil." —*Matthew 6:13

We face a very clear and present danger in our generation. Behind the scenes a battle is being fought for the very hearts and lives of men, women, and children across the planet. This invisible war is being waged between the forces of evil and the forces of good, between God Himself and a created being known as Satan.

We, as believers, are in this battle and we're in it

to the very end. We are not tourists on a vacation in this world if we're following Jesus. We are soldiers on a mission for Him. And the only way to win this war is to prepare and to pray.

Jesus said in John 16:33, *"In this world you will have tribulation."* But then He added, *"but be of good cheer for I have overcome the world."* He taught us to pray in order to overcome the temptation of the enemy. When we pray, we are protecting our faith, our future, and our families.

When faced with temptation, our natural reaction is often to run to the world for our solutions or we fight the best we can with our flesh. We do everything *except* pray and ask God to deliver us! In these times, we must remember that we are fighting a *spiritual* battle that can only be won with the *spiritual weapons* God has provided. God has promised deliverance for His children if we pray.

Maybe you're in the throes of temptation right now and you're tempted to compromise your purity. You're in a test of your faith. Perhaps you are tempted by unhealthy habits or to say words that are better left unsaid. What do you do? How do you pray so that you can resist the enemy and overcome opposition in your life?

Turn to God for strength in times of temptation and realize that He understands the pressure you are experiencing. 1 Corinthians 10:13 assures us that, *"No temptation has overtaken you that is not common to man. God is faithful, and he will not let you be tempted beyond your ability, but with the temptation he will also provide the way of escape, that you may be able to endure it."*

In a world filled with temptation, we have a stronghold against the enemy because our God is a deliverer. He specializes in deliverance. Our Savior is a mighty warrior who has conquered sin, death, and hell! And we can defeat the enemy with the Word of God, the sword of the Spirit. We can resist temptation in the power of Jesus Christ!

There are all kinds of attacks in our generation—attacks of men and attacks of ideologies. But behind all of them is the evil one. Remember to pray daily for the power of Jesus Christ in your life to deliver you!

Think about the temptations surrounding you and the ones you love. Use your prayer time today to pray for protection from and strength during temptation.

DAY 24:
STRENGTH IN TIMES OF WEAKNESS

Trust in him at all times, O people; pour out
your heart before him; God is a refuge for us.
—Psalm 62:8

It is often in the very toughest of times and trials that God brings us to a crisis of faith, and it's through that experience that we begin to pray. I've heard it said that, "when you're swept off your feet, get on your knees."

I experienced such a time in 2009 when I was diagnosed with prostate cancer. Me—a relatively young guy in excellent health with energy to spare. I never imagined that the word *cancer* would be attached to my life. And yet it was.

While I made it through surgery without incident, recovery nearly did me in. I was exhausted. I was fearful. I was weak and despondent. I wondered if I would ever get better.

For many months I prayed to God for healing and for hope. Meanwhile, week after week, I crawled into the pulpit to deliver my weekly sermon, sustained only by the prayerful persistence that connected my heart to God's.

Strangely during this time of pain and weakness, more than any other point in my life, I became utterly convinced of the power of prayer. Though I was wobbly and wounded, the more I pursued interaction with my heavenly

Father, the more divine strength I sensed in my life. The more I knocked on the doors of heaven, the more I found God ready and willing to carry the burden I bore.

Whatever broken conditions you are facing today—in your marriage, your home, your family, through a child that's wandered away, or the collapse of a career—it is so often pain that drives us to dependence upon God.

How many times through our pain do we discover our purpose? How many times through our pain do we discover power? 2 Corinthians 12:9 reminds us that God's grace is sufficient and that His power is made perfect through our weaknesses.

I've always loved the definition of prayer as "linking our nothingness to God's almightiness."

When we're wrestling our way through tragedy or wringing our hands over a cupboard that's bare, God says, "It is I who can supply what you need. Just come to Me and ask."

With God all of your cares will be cared for. All that is His will be yours. Through prayer you can experience the delightful nearness of God and lean into His warm embrace.

Today, stay before God in prayer until He communicates with your spirit. Surrender your weaknesses to Him and exchange them for supernatural strength.

DAY 25:
GREATER LOVE FOR OTHERS

And I pray that you, being rooted and established
in love, may have power, together with
all the Lord's holy people, to grasp how wide
and long and high and deep is the love of Christ.
—Ephesians 3:17–18

Ephesians 1:15–21 explains that it is through prayer that we see with the eyes of our hearts. The apostle Paul's hope was that through *"having the eyes of your hearts enlightened, that you may know what is the hope to which he has called you, what are the riches of his glorious inheritance*

in the saints, and what is the immeasurable greatness of his power toward us who believe."

So how can we open the "eyes of our hearts"?

First, by realizing the value of the gift we've been given in Christ. We have already seen that God's grace and forgiveness are available to all who call upon Him. We are in God's eternal debt because we have been forgiven, fully and freely. It's illustrated so powerfully, so beautifully in the story of the Prodigal Son in Luke 15. When that son who had rebelled and wasted his entire inheritance came home, his father ran to him and welcomed him home. And in the greatest redemption story of all time, Jesus took the debt that was against us and nailed it to the cross. You're never more like Jesus than when you're extending the forgiveness and the love and the grace that He has given you to another person.

Second, we can see with the eyes of our hearts by praying for Christ's love to fill us. It is a characteristic of a person who knows Jesus and has experienced unconditional love, that they will extend that love to others. When your prayer life is active and full, when you are communing daily with God, you will begin to see others as God sees them. I challenge you to pray that sometime—the next time you find yourself angry, frustrated, or disappointed with someone, pray, "Lord, help me to see this person as You see him."

The next time you are compelled to harbor bitterness or respond in anger, pause and soak in the gravity of God's unconditional love for you. *"Greater love has no one than this, that someone lay down his life for his friends,"* John

15:13 says. Jesus died so that you and I could live a life worthy of the debt He paid.

There are two more important verses I want to point out from John: *"Beloved, let us love one another, for love is from God, and whoever loves has been born of God and knows God. Anyone who does not love does not know God, because God is love"* (1 John 4:7-–8). *"By this all people will know that you are my disciples, if you have love for one another"* (John 13:35). Is God's love flowing from your life?

Would someone recognize you as a believer in Christ by the love you have shown to others this week? If you have a little work to do in this area, make your prayer today centered upon love. How can you show it more to those around you? Ask God for help in this area.

DAY 26:
A SPIRIT OF GRATITUDE

The joy of the Lord is your strength!
—Nehemiah 8:10

Gratitude has been described as the healthiest of all human emotions. Think about it: if you live with a grateful heart, if you live with praise and thanksgiving to God, it counteracts any toxic, negative emotions in your life. It elevates your spirit!

Any time I start feeling down, depleted, and tired, do you know what I do? I start praising

Jesus! I start rejoicing in Jesus, that my sins are forgiven, that He's given me His Word and His truth to guide me, that I have a future and a hope with Him. I rejoice in the fact that the Spirit of God lives in me. I celebrate the fact that I've got a Christian family and friends who love me. When I use prayer to express my gratefulness to God, He begins lifting my spirits, because His joy becomes my strength. And His strength allows me to stand strong in the power of His might!

Because of this joy, I have strength today that comes from God. I have the strength of God, the power of Jesus in my life. I've got as much energy as I ever had. It's not because of me; it's because of Him and His love flowing through my life!

Now some of you may be thinking, *Well, that*

sounds nice but I'm not standing; I'm in bed, I'm sick, I can't even get out of the retirement home, or I can't get out of this hospital. Even when you can't physically stand, the joy of the Lord can be your strength. In spite of your suffering, and even in your pain, God gives you a reason to be grateful.

Sometimes we just need a change of perspective. And that's why God says that we should begin thinking and praying with thanksgiving in our hearts. A prayerful life allows us to rest and reflect upon the goodness of God. First Thessalonians 5:18 says *"Give thanks in all circumstances, for this is the will of God in Jesus Christ for you."* Not because of all things, but in all things we can give thanks.

Don't stop celebrating what Christ has done for you. Rejoice in the Lord! Pray with gratitude!

Pray with thanksgiving! Because I'm telling you even if you die, it's only going to get better! *"To live is Christ, and to die is gain!"* (Philippians 1:21).

Every breath you breathe and every beat of your heart is a gift from God. Pray today for the joy of the Lord to fill your heart so that you can see your life with new perspective. Ask God to help you see the many reasons you have to be grateful.

DAY 27:
THE ANTIDOTE FOR ANXIETY

"Do not be anxious about anything but in everything by prayer and supplication with thanksgiving let your requests be known to God."
—Philippians 4:6

In Philippians chapter 4 God reveals the antidote for anxiety. His prescription in the midst of our pain, fear, and uncertainty is always prayer.

It is amazing to me that, when Paul gave us these words inspired by the Holy Spirit, he was not on a Mediterranean cruise on his way to hang out on the beach. No, he was in prison in Rome, and he was writing to Christians at Philippi, who would experience persecution and pressure in their lives.

While we may never experience the confines of an actual prison, there are prisons of other kinds—prisons of personal pain, suffering, and sickness. There is the bondage of bitterness. Some of you may feel you are in a dungeon of depression. Others are behind walls of loneliness and isolation, fettered by fear and feeling chained by their circumstances.

It's true that the Apostle Paul was in prison, but he wasn't there alone. In the previous verse he said, *"The Lord is at hand"*(4:5). Jesus promised that His presence would always be with us through His Spirit. This is the reason that we can rejoice in *all* things; not in our circumstances, but in Christ Himself.

Prayer is the cure for every worry. It should never be our last chance, but always our first choice. Don't wait to pray for something until you've "worried it to death." If you are awake at night, unable to sleep because you can't get your worries off your mind, don't toss and turn. Just turn to the Lord.

Worry is assuming responsibility that God never intended for us to have. Worry is saying, "God, I can't trust You to provide for my needs." But Jesus said, *"Therefore, I tell you, do not be anxious about your life, what you will eat or what you will drink."* He said, *"Look at the birds of the air: they neither sow nor reap nor gather into barns, and yet your heavenly Father feeds them. Are you not of more value than they? And which of you by being*

anxious can add a single hour to his span of life?"
(Matthew 6:25–27). We don't need to fret about
our future because it's all in God's hands.

Worry never solved a problem. Worry never dried
a tear. In fact, the word worry comes from an Old
English word meaning "to choke or to strangle."
That's a word picture of what worry does to us—it
is emotional strangulation! Worry, fear, anxiety
will suffocate and paralyze us, rendering us
useless for God's kingdom. Don't let that happen
in your life. Give your worries to God in prayer.
The beginning of worry is the end of faith. But
the beginning of true faith is the end of worry.

**What is causing you to worry today? Write it in
a prayer to Jesus and replace your worry with
the peace He offers.**

DAY 28:
PEACE IN ALL CIRCUMSTANCES

"Peace I leave with you; my peace I give to you.
Not as the world gives do I give to you."
—John 14:27

In yesterday's reading, we saw how worry and anxiety can be defeated through prayer. In the very next verse in Scripture (Philippians 4:7), Jesus tells us that when we've given our anxiety and our prayers to the Lord, we will receive the gift of peace: *"and the peace of God, which passes all understanding, will guard your hearts and minds in Christ Jesus."*

We receive the Lord's peace when we pray.

Literally, God's peace descends upon us and takes action! It guards our hearts and our minds. Now maybe you're thinking, *Well, I lost my peace.* No, you didn't. Jesus keeps your peace. You can't lose your peace if Jesus is keeping it, if He's guarding it. Isaiah 26:3 says that God will, *"keep him in perfect peace whose mind is stayed on you because he trusts in You."*

Live in prayer and you will live in peace! There will be quietness and confidence in our lives because instead of getting "worked up" over life's problems we are choosing to "pray them down."

When we continue reading in Philippians 4, we are given more advice for experiencing peace in all circumstances: *"What you have learned and received and heard and seen in me—practice these things, and the God of peace will be with you."*

Prayer not only gives us peace but it arms us with a conquering spirit, an overcoming spirit! We begin to believe again! We believe to trust the promises of God again! We begin to stand in the strength that is our God when we pray!

If you have never read the biblical story of Shadrach, Meshach, and Abednego in its entirety, I would encourage you to do so.[6] These three friends, who refused to bow down to King Nebuchadnezzar's idols, were sentenced to a fiery death. Facing a horrible fate, they stood in peace, placing their complete trust in Almighty God.

To the astonishment of the King, when he looked into the furnace, instead of three sets of ashes, he saw four living beings! Walking in that fire beside his faithful followers was the living presence of Jesus Himself! You see, Jesus doesn't always keep us out of the fire, but He will always get in the fire with us. When we love and trust Him, God brings His presence and His peace to every area of our lives.

Has peace escaped you? Reclaim it today by praying Philippians 4:7. When our eternity is secure in Jesus, we can live in peace regardless of our circumstances.

DAY 29:
THE OPPORTUNITY
TO BLESS OTHERS

*Praise be to the God and Father of our Lord Jesus
Christ, the Father of compassion and God of all
comfort, who comforts us in all our troubles, so
that we can comfort those in any trouble with the
comfort we ourselves have received from God.*
—2 Corinthians 1:3–4

I believe the most important lesson I've ever
learned regarding prayer is that it is far
better to *be* an answer to prayer than to get an
answer to prayer. Why? Because God wants to

6 See Daniel 3:1-30

answer prayers through us, according to His power at work within us.

When you start praying for others you allow yourself to be a channel of blessing. God has blessed us that we would be a blessing to others.

If God has blessed you with a house, you can share your hospitality with others who need it. If God has blessed you with a full table, you can share food with those who need it. If God has given you an overflowing bank account, share what God has given to help reach those who need Jesus. Luke 12:48 reminds us that, *"To whom much is given, much is required."*

The Bible is filled with examples of God's using willing servants to convey His blessings to others. Remember Moses? Out there in the desert, he was praying for the children of Israel as the Israelites were praying in Egypt. And God came to Moses in that burning bush and said, "I have heard their cry." Then God told Moses that he was going to be used by Him to answer the Israelites' prayers.

While it is wonderful to pray, "Lord, help that missionary," at some point God's response may be, "Now I want you to go and share the Good News!" If you're praying, "Lord, save that lost person," listen carefully because God may put your feet to your prayers and say, "You go and tell your friend about Me." Are you willing to be an answer to prayer?

So many people today are looking for churches to bless them. Instead of looking for some place to bless us, why don't we look for someplace to *be* a blessing, to meet people's needs? There will always be people who take more out of life than they put into it. But the Christian, the servant of Jesus Christ, should continually endeavor to put more back in to life and to God's kingdom than they've taken out.

One of the greatest joys in my life is when somebody says to me, "Jack, you were an answer to my prayer. You met a need in my life. You helped me." When that happens to any of us, the glory belongs to God.

As you begin your day, ask God to show you a specific way in which you can bless someone today. Keep the eyes of your heart open for opportunities God will place on your heart.

DAY 30:
TRUE SURRENDER

I beseech you, or I beg you, brothers, by the mercies
of God, that you present or offer your bodies
as a living sacrifice, holy and acceptable
unto God, which is your reasonable service.
And do not be conformed to this world, but be
transformed by the renewing of your mind, that
you may prove what is that good and perfect and
acceptable will of God." —Romans 12:1

S *urrender:* it's a word we don't like very
much because it speaks of capitulation or
compromise. Surrender implies loss, and in

a world that glorifies winners we don't want to have anything to do with that. And yet God says to the believer, *surrender your life to Me.* In this sense, surrender involves complete dedication and consecration. True surrender involves getting off the throne of my life and saying, "Lord, take charge. Lord, You take command of my life."

God is not a tyrant. He is our loving, holy and heavenly Father. We can trust Him with our families, with our future, and with our fears. Indeed, the only natural response to the beautiful gift of His grace is full surrender, allowing Him to be King in all areas of life. Our dreams and desires, our longings and wants— God wants to be Lord over all. This type of surrender is not limiting, but liberating!

Mary, the mother of Jesus, knew this truth well. When she, a virgin, was told that she would give birth to the Savior of the world, she was more than a little shocked. *"How can these things be?"* she asked. But despite her perplexed state, she surrendered to God: *"Behold, I am the servant of the Lord; let it be to me according to your word"* (Luke 1:38).

My prayer for each of us is that we would respond in the same way. Sure, we may not always understand the what, when, how, and why of God's perfect will for our lives, but of this I am utterly sure: We can trust God to lead us well. God has a wonderful plan for our lives! When we give ourselves unreservedly to Him, He will do His very best for us. Jeremiah 29:11 says, *"I know the plans that I have for you, says the Lord, plans not to harm you but to give you a future and a hope."*

The fact is, if we don't surrender to Jesus we'll surrender to something else—to chaos or confusion, to the opinions of others, or to habits that we can't control. We will surrender to something or someone.

Several years ago, I discovered a powerful little verse that I carry with me wherever I go: *"So whether we are at home or away, we make it our aim to please him"* (2 Corinthians 5:9). We please God with our laid-down lives.

Will you surrender your life to the Lord Jesus Christ? Don't let fear or pride stop you from doing so. If you are ready to fully submit to God's leadership and lordship today, record your decision on a Prayer Page along with today's date.

CONCLUSION

It is my sincere hope that this book has been read through, prayed through, and filled with your personal conversations with the Lord. I encourage you to look back through this book as God answers your prayers or when He gives you specific insight into situations for which you have prayed.

I want to leave you with an incredibly powerful verse from Ephesians that really sums up the blessings of a prayer-filled life:

"For this reason I bow my knees before the Father, from whom every family in heaven and on earth

is named, that according to the riches of his glory he may grant you to be strengthened with power through his Spirit in your inner being, so that Christ may dwell in your hearts through faith—that you, being rooted and grounded in love, may have strength to comprehend with all the saints what is the breadth and length and height and depth, and to know the love of Christ that surpasses knowledge, that you may be filled with all the fullness of God. Now to him who is able to do far more abundantly than all that we ask or think, according to the power at work within us, to Him be glory in the church and in Christ Jesus throughout all generations forever and ever, Amen." —Ephesians 3:14–21

May these 30 days of prayer serve as a spark to ignite flames of passion within your heart—passion for a growing, prayerful relationship

with God. My own prayers will be joined with yours as we pray for God's will to be done on earth and as we pray for leaders and loved ones. Our hearts will unite with other believers as we pray boldly, persistently, and with humility to spare. May we all pray with a conquering spirit, knowing we'll rise believing once more. Our knuckles may become bruised from knocking, but the rewards are impossible to deny.

—Jack Graham

PRAYER PAGE

Today's Date: _____

My Prayer: _____

_____

_____

_____

_____

_____

_____

_____

_____

_____

_____

_____

_____

_____

_____

_____

PRAYER PAGE

Today's Date: _____

My Prayer: _____

_____

_____

_____

_____

_____

_____

_____

_____

_____

_____

_____

_____

_____

_____

_____

PRAYER PAGE

Today's Date: _____

My Prayer: _____

_____

_____

_____

_____

_____

_____

_____

_____

_____

_____

_____

_____

_____

_____

PRAYER PAGE

Today's Date: _____

My Prayer: _____

_____

_____

_____

_____

_____

_____

_____

_____

_____

_____

_____

_____

_____

_____

_____

PRAYER PAGE

Today's Date: _____

My Prayer: _____

_____

_____

_____

_____

_____

_____

_____

_____

_____

_____

_____

_____

_____

_____

_____

PRAYER PAGE

Today's Date: _____

My Prayer: _____

_____

_____

_____

_____

_____

_____

_____

_____

_____

_____

_____

_____

_____

_____

_____

_____

PRAYER PAGE

Today's Date: _____

My Prayer: _____

_____

_____

_____

_____

_____

_____

_____

_____

_____

_____

_____

_____

_____

_____

PRAYER PAGE

Today's Date: _____

My Prayer: _____

_____

_____

_____

_____

_____

_____

_____

_____

_____

_____

_____

_____

_____

_____

_____

PRAY FOR THE 7 CENTERS OF INFLUENCE

GOVERNMENT

(1 Timothy 2:1–4)

Pray for our local, state, and national leaders asking God to grant them wisdom, discernment, and hearts that are open to His leading.

CHURCH

(Colossians 2:6–8)

Pray for the churches and church leaders throughout our nation and in your community. Ask God to preserve and protect them as He inspires and empowers them to equip His saints for the work of ministry, for the building up of the Church, and for the spreading of the Gospel.

MILITARY
(2 Chronicles 32:6–8)

Pray for our military and its leaders. Pray for God to grant courage, protection, and strength for our service men and women, and their families, as they serve our country.

FAMILY
(Mark 3:25)

Pray for families in our nation, in your state, and throughout your community. Pray with passion for the Lord to protect and to strengthen marriages, encourage parents toward His priorities, heal relationships, and secure His values in their homes.

EDUCATION
(Proverbs 2:3–6)

Pray for God's presence in our schools, colleges, and universities. Ask Him to select teachers and administrators who honor His statutes, protect our children, and inspire them to discover their God-given calling.

BUSINESS
(Exodus 31:3–4)

Pray for divine intervention in our national, state, and local economies. Ask that God raise up godly business leaders and create industry to provide honest employment and generous provision for individuals and families in each community.

MEDIA AND ENTERTAINMENT
(Philippians 4:8)

Pray for Christian influence in the media industry, from movies, television, and radio stations, to newspaper and magazine publishers. Ask the Lord to provide godly men and women to work in and influence the media throughout the nation, your state and in every city.